A Sandwich

by Owen Patterson
illustrated by Zahira Khan

Practice Pre-Decodable 8

McGraw Hill Education

Bothell, WA • Chicago, IL • Columbus, OH • New York, NY

MHEonline.com

Send all inquiries to:
McGraw-Hill Education
8787 Orion Place
Columbus, OH 43240

ISBN: 978-0-02-140447-6
MHID: 0-02-140447-X

Printed in China.

9 10 11 12 13 DSS 27 26 25 24 23

He had 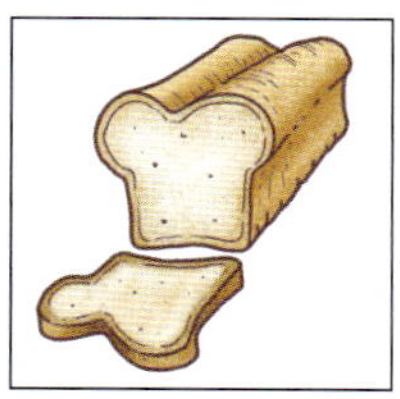 .

bread

He had  .

ham

He had  .

cheese

He had a  .

tomato

He had  .

pickles

He had a .

sandwich